THE TRIUMPHS OF PETRARCH

THE TRIUMPHS OF PETRARCH

TRANSLATED BY ERNEST HATCH WILKINS

Drawings by Virgil Burnett

THE UNIVERSITY OF CHICAGO PRESS

Library of Congress Catalog Card Number: 62-19622

THE UNIVERSITY OF CHICAGO PRESS, CHICAGO & LONDON
The University of Toronto Press, Toronto 5, Canada

PREFACE

The six *Triumphs* of Petrarch constituted the most triumphant poem of the early Renaissance: for a hundred years and more they outshone both the *Divine Comedy* and Petrarch's own sonnets and *canzoni*. Their extraordinary immediate success came to them because to their first readers they seemed at once familiar and novel—familiar in their concern with love and in their visionary character, novel in their vivid evocation of dimly remembered persons and processions of the ancient world.

The pictorial character of the *Triumphs* made them at once a welcome resource both for painters, who depicted them on *cassoni*, on panels, on canvases, and in frescoes, and for workers in other media, who treated the Triumph theme in woodcuts, in engravings, in bas-reliefs, in bronze plaques, on armor, in stained glass, and in tapestries.

The *Triumphs* have then a historic cultural importance: they possess enduring values as well. They do not equal the lyrics of Petrarch in poetic excellence, and there are passages that are of little interest to a modern reader. But the sequence of the later *Triumphs* has grandeur—fame triumphs over death, time over fame, eternity over time; many lines and tercets are of fine quality; the end of the canto on the death of Laura is deservedly famous for its serene beauty; and the canto that tells of Laura's appearance to Petrarch in a vision, with its long and tender conversation, in the course of which Laura admits an understanding

and a love never confessed elsewhere, is perhaps the most re-
markable personal passage that Petrarch ever wrote.

The several *Triumphs* were not written continuously, or as
parts of a single poem. The first two were written, probably
within the years 1340–44, as a twofold poem, complete in itself,
and without any thought that other *Triumphs* were to follow.
The death of Laura in 1348, however, led Petrarch to the writ-
ing of the *Triumph of Death;* and he began work on the *Triumph
of Fame* soon afterward. The last two *Triumphs* were written
toward the end of his life.

While he frequently retouched individual passages he never
made the *Triumphs* into a finished and unified series. Some
scholars believe that if he had done so he would have omitted
the cantos that are here—and usually—treated as the second
canto of the *Triumph of Love* and the second canto of the *Triumph of Death.* There are variant endings for the third canto of
the *Triumph of Love.* In addition to the twelve cantos here
translated there remains one other complete canto, which was
written as a first canto for the *Triumph of Fame,* but was soon
replaced by what are now the first and second cantos of that
Triumph. It is clear also that Petrarch was not satisfied with the
third canto of that same *Triumph:* it is obviously incomplete as
it stands, and there has recently been discovered a fragmentary
draft of a canto that was designed as a replacement for it. There
exists also a short fragment of what was apparently intended to
be a draft for the opening lines of the *Triumph of Death.*

The Triumphs are written in *terza rima,* the metrical form
devised by Dante for his *Comedy.*

The best edition of the Italian text of the *Triumphs* is that con-
tained in Ezio Chiòrboli's edition of *Le rime sparse e i Trionfi*

(Bari, 1930). The best notes are those of Carlo Calcaterra, in his edition of *I Trionfi* (Turin, 1927), which contains also an excellent introduction and an index of personal and place names. Good notes are to be found also in Andrea Moschetti's edition of *Il Canzoniere e i Trionfi* (Milan, 1908), and in the edition of the *Rime, Trionfi e Poesie latine* edited by Ferdinando Neri and others (Milan and Naples, 1951).

There have been only two previous English translations of the whole series of the *Triumphs:* the first, by Henry Parker, Lord Morley, was published in 1554; the second, by the Reverend Henry Boyd, was first published in 1807.

My translation, which is based upon Chiòrboli's text, retains the tercet structure of the original, but does not attempt to preserve the Italian rhyme scheme.

NOTE ON PRONUNCIATION

The pronunciation of certain relatively unfamiliar Latin names may be indicated thus: Aesacus (*Ae* as *É*), Anaxímenes, Antísthenes, Céyx (*y* as *i*), Demóphoön, Dicaeárchus (*cae* as *ke*), Halcýone (*y* as *í*), Oenóne (*Oe* as *E*), Stratónica, Typhoeus (*oe* as *é*).

The pronunciation of certain Italian place names may be indicated thus: Bárbaro, Íschia (*ch* as *k*), Lípari, Strómboli.

In the Provençal names Daniel and Rudel the stress is on the last syllable. In Alvernhe the *nh* is pronounced like the usual French *gn* or the Spanish *ñ*.

CONTENTS

THE TRIUMPH OF LOVE

I

THE SEASON when my sighing is renewed
Had come, stirring the memory of that day
Whereon my love and suffering began.

    The sun was warming one and the other horn
Of Taurus, and Tithonus' youthful bride
Sped in the coolness to her wonted station;

    Springtime and love and scorn and tearfulness
Again had brought me to that Vale Enclosed
Where from my heart its heavy burdens fall;

    And there, amid the grasses, faint from weeping,
O'ercome with sleep, I saw a spacious light
Wherein were ample grief and little joy.

    A leader, conquering and supreme, I saw,
Such as triumphal chariots used to bear
To glorious honor on the Capitol.

    Never had I beheld a sight like this—
Thanks to the sorry age in which I live,
Bereft of valor, and o'erfilled with pride—

And I, desirous evermore to learn,
Lifted my weary eyes, and gazed upon
This scene, so wondrous and so beautiful.

    Four steeds I saw, whiter than whitest snow,
And on a fiery car a cruel youth
With bow in hand and arrows at his side.

    No fear had he, nor armor wore, nor shield,
But on his shoulders he had two great wings
Of a thousand hues; his body was all bare.

    And round about were mortals beyond count:
Some of them were but captives, some were slain,
And some were wounded by his pungent arrows.

    Eager for tidings, I moved toward the throng,
So that I came near to becoming one
Of those who by his hand had lost their lives.

    Then I moved closer still, to see if any
I recognized among the pressing host
Following the king ne'er satisfied with tears.

    None did I seem to know; for if there were
Among them any I had known, their looks
Were changed by death or fierce captivity.

    Toward me there came a spirit somewhat less
Distressed than the others, calling me by name,
And saying: "These are the gains of those who love!"

Wond'ring, I said to him: "How knowest thou
My face? for thee I cannot recognize."
And he: "The heavy bonds that weigh me down
 Prevent thee, and the dimness of the air.
But I am a friend to thee, and I was born,
As thou, within the land of Tuscany."

 His words and the noble manner of his speech
Revealed to me what his changed looks had hidden.
So we took seat in a high and open place;

 And he began: "Long have I thought to see
Thee here among us: from thine early years
Thy life foretold that this would be thy fate."

 " 'Twas even so; but then the toils of love
Dismayed me so that I abandoned them,
My garments and my heart already rent."

 When I had spoken, and when he had heard
My answer, not without a smile he said:
"Oh my son, what a flame is lit for thee!"

 I did not understand him then, but now
So surely in my head his words are fixed
That ne'er more deeply was aught writ in marble.

 And in the boldness of my youth—when mind
And tongue are quick in utterance—I asked:
"Pray, of your courtesy, what folk are these?"

7

"Ere long," he answered, "thou thyself shalt know,
Thyself being one of them: thou knowest not
How firm a bond is being made for thee.

    Thy looks shall fade, and white shall be thy hair,
Before the bond I speak of is unloosed,
However much thy neck and feet rebel.

    And yet, to satisfy thy youthful wish,
I'll answer, telling of our master first,
Who rives us thus of life and liberty.

    For this is he whom the world calleth Love:
Bitter, thou see'st, as thou wilt see more clearly
When he shall be thy lord, as he is ours—

    Gentle in youth and fierce as he grows old,
As who makes trial knows, and thou shalt know
In less than a thousand years, I prophesy.

    Idleness gave him birth, and wantonness,
And he was nursed by sweet and gentle thoughts,
And a vain folk made him their lord and god.

    Some of his captives die forthwith; and some
More pitilessly ruled, live out their lives
Under a thousand chains and a thousand keys.

    He who so lordly and so proud appears,
First of us all, is Caesar, whom in Egypt
Cleopatra bound, amid the flowers and grass.

Now over him there is triumph; and 'tis well,
Since he, though conqueror of the world, was vanquished,
That Love, who vanquished him, should have the glory.

Next comes his son—he too was one who loved,
Although more nobly—Caesar Augustus he,
Who took his Livia from her generous spouse.

The third is Nero, pitiless and unjust:
See how he marches full of wrath and scorn.
A woman conquered him, strong though he seems.

See the good Marcus, worthy of all praise,
His tongue and heart full of philosophy—
And yet Faustina bends him to her will.

Those two who walk in fear and in suspicion
Are Dionysius and that Alexander
Whose jealous thoughts led him unto his death.

The next is he who by Antandros wept
Creusa's death, and took another bride
From that same prince who slew Evander's son.

Thou wilt have heard of one who would not yield
To a stepmother's passionate pursuit
And gained through flight escape from her entreaties:

And yet his chaste and rightful steadfastness
Brought him to death: for to such hatred turned
The love of Phaedra, terrible and malign.

Herself she slew, perchance avenging thus
Theseus, Hippolytus, and Ariadne,
Who, as thou know'st, sped, loving, to her death.

Blaming another, one condemns oneself:
For he who takes delight in fraudulence
May not lament if he too be deceived.

Behold then Theseus, captive, though so famed,
Led between sisters twain who both met death:
One set her love on him, he loved the other.

With him is Hercules: for all his strength
Love captured him. Achilles follows on,
Who in his loving met with bitter grief.

That is Demophoon, and that is Phyllis;
And that is Jason: with him is Medea,
Who followed him, and Love, o'er land and sea,

To father and to brother pitiless,
And toward her lover wild and fierce, as though
She might be thus more worthy of his love.

Hypsipyle comes after, and bemoans
The barbarous love that reft her of her own.
And then comes she who bears the vaunt of beauty,

The shepherd with her from whose fateful sight
Of her fair face came the tempestuous storms
That with their raging overturned the world.

And then Oenone thou may'st hear lament
For Paris; and for Helen, Menelaus.
Hermione for her Orestes calls,
    Laodamia for Protesilaus.
Argia, faithfully, for Polynices,
Unlike Amphiaraus' covetous wife.
    Hark to the sighs and weeping, hark to the cries
Of these poor loving ones, who gave their souls
Into the power of him who leads them thus.
    Nor could I ever name them all to thee:
Not only human folk but gods are here,
Filling the shadows of the myrtle grove.
    See lovely Venus, and with her see Mars,
His feet and arms and neck laden with chains.
Yonder are Pluto and Proserpina.
    Behold the jealous Juno, and the blond
Apollo, who once scorned the youthful bow
That dealt him such a wound in Thessaly.
    What shall I say? To put it briefly, then,
All Varro's gods are here as prisoners,
And, burdened with innumerable bonds,
    Before the chariot goes Jupiter."

II

Weary with gazing, yet unsatisfied,
I turned now this way and now that, and saw
Sights time will not suffice me to relate.

My mind was moving on from thought to thought
When it was drawn to two who side by side
Were walking, and together gently weeping.

'Twas their strange dress that made me notice them;
Their foreign speech I could not understand
Until my friend interpreted for me.

And when I knew their names, I went to them
With more assurance: one of them for Rome
Felt friendliness—the other nought but hate.

To one I spoke: "O noble Masinissa,
For Scipio's sake, and your companion's sake,
Be not offended, prithee, by my words."

Looking at me, he said: "Fain would I know
Who thou mayst be, that so unerringly
Both of my dear affections hast discerned."

"I am not worthy to be known," I said,
"By such a knower: this slight flame of mine
Hath not the power to cast its light so far.

Thy royal fame extends throughout the world,
And binds to thee with the fair bond of love
Folk who have never seen thee, nor shall see.

Now tell me, as ye hope for peace to come
(I pointed to their Leader), who ye are,
Ye twain, who seem to be of wondrous faith."

"Thy tongue, that is so ready with my name,
Proves that thou know'st already who we are,"
Said he, "but I will speak to ease my grief.

To that great man so heartily allied
Was I that not e'en Laelius loved him more:
Where'er his banners led, I followed them.

Fortune to him was ever generous,
Yet not beyond the measure of the worth
That filled his soul past all comparison.

After the Roman arms so gloriously
Had spread their victories into the West,
There Love found us and joined us, who are one.

Never was sweeter flame in two hearts lit,
Nor shall be. Nights too few, alas,
Were for our great desires so brief and scarce

(In vain, for us, our solemn marriage vow)
That all the goodly reasons for our love
And the sacred bond itself came soon to nought.

For Scipio—worthier than all the world—
With holy words bade us to separate,
Nor could he heed the pity of our sighing.

And though it brought and brings me bitter dole,
Yet virtue shone in him so marvelously
That one is blind who cannot see that sun.

    To those who love, high justice is high doom;
And thus the verdict of so great a friend
Stood like a rock to thwart enduring love.

    Father in honor, he to me; a son
In love; in years a brother: I obeyed,
With breaking heart and countenance distressed.

    So then this dear one came unto her death:
For, being subject to an alien foe,
She chose to die rather than live a slave.

    And I of mine own grief was minister,
For she so passionately entreated me
That I, who suffered that she might not suffer,

    Sent her the poison—with such sorrowing thought
As she well knows and I remember well,
And thou mayst know, if thou too knowest love.

    All my inheritance from my bride was grief:
Herself, and every happiness and hope,
I chose to lose, to keep my faith with her.

    But see now if thou findest in this dance
Aught that is worthy of note, for the time is short
And thou hast more to see than the day can show."

O'erwhelmed with pity, thinking of the brief
Time granted to the love of such a pair,
My heart was like to snow that melts i' the sun,

When, as they started on again, I heard:
"This man is friendly in himself, I ween,
Yet for all Romans have I nought but hate."

"Put now thy heart in peace, O Sophonisba,
For by our hands the Carthage that was thine
Hath fallen thrice, and will not rise again."

But she replied: "Tell me another tale:
Africa wept; but Rome had little cause
For laughter—as your histories will confess."

Then he who had loved both her and us moved on,
Smiling, with her, amid the mighty throng,
And presently they passed beyond my sight.

As one who travels by a doubtful road
And stops at every step, and looks about
And ponders, hesitant and slow to move,

E'en so the train of lovers made my steps
Unsure and halting: for I sought to know
With what a fire each burned, and how intense.

I saw one to the left and out of line,
Like to a man who something seeks and finds
Wherefrom both shame and joy may come to him.

To give to another man one's own dear spouse:
Oh utmost love, unheard-of courtesy!
So that she too ashamed and joyous seemed

    For the exchange: and all three onward moved
Talking together of their cherished loves,
And sighing for the land of Syria.

    I went to the three spirits, who together
Were following a pathway of their own,
And to the first I said, "I pray thee, wait!"

    Hearing the accents of my Latin speech,
Troubled in countenance, he stayed his steps;
And then, as though perceiving my desire,

    He said: "I am Seleucus, and this is
My son Antiochus, who warred with you—
But right avails not against greater strength.

    And she who is with us was first my wife
And then was his: for lest he die of love
To him I gave her, as in our land I might.

    Stratonica she is named; and as thou see'st
We are not divided: by that very sign
Our love is manifest as strong and firm.

    She was content to leave me, queen no more;
I to leave my delight; and he his life:
Each thought another far the worthier.

He would have perished in the flower of youth
But for the wisdom of his good physician,
Who understood the cause of his distress.

Loving in silence, he was near to death—
Constrained by love, silently virtuous—
Mine was paternal love, that succored him."

These words he spoke: then turned and started on,
Like to a man moved by a new intent,
So quickly that I scarce could say farewell.

After the spirit passed beyond my sight,
Leaving me pensive, I moved onward, sighing,
My heart still meditating on his words,

Until a voice said to me: "Give no more
Heed to this single thought: there is much else
To see, and, as thou know'st, the time is short."

More were the lovers here, captive and bare,
Than all the soldiers Xerxes led to Greece—
The host extending farther than my sight.

Of many tongues and many lands they were.
Hardly of one in a thousand did I learn
The name; and of those few my tale shall be.

Perseus was there, from whom I sought to know
Of the Ethiopian maiden whom he loved,
Andromeda, dark of eye and dark of hair.

There the vain lover was who through desire
Of his own mirrored beauty was undone,
Poor only in that he possessed too much—
　　A blossom he became, that bears no fruit,
And she who, loving him, a floating voice
Became, her gentle body turned to stone.
　　There too was Iphis, quick to his own ill,
Who, loving vainly, hated his own life;
And many more who knew like suffering,
　　Folk crossed in love who had no wish to live.
Moderns I saw among them, but to tell
Their unrenownèd names I will not stay.
　　Those two were there whom Love companions made
Forever, Ceyx and Halcyone,
Nest-builders by the sea in winter's calm.
　　Near to these twain I beheld Aesacus
Seeking Hesperia—now on rocky shore,
Now under sea, now flying through mid air.
　　The cruel daughter of Nisus there I saw,
Swift in her flight; and Atalanta running,
By golden apples vanquished, and the beauty
　　Of her Hippomenes: his rivals all
Lost both the fateful race and their own lives,
And he alone could boast of victory.

Among these vain and fabled loves I saw
Acis, with Galatea in his arms,
And Polyphemus roaring in his wrath.
    I saw the sea-borne Glaucus in the throng
Without her who alone was dear to him,
And heard him name one who had loved too well;
    Canens and Picus, erst a Latian king
And now a bird—and she who wrought the change
Left him his name and his fair royal robe.
    I saw Egeria weeping; and beheld
Scylla transformed into a rugged rock
That menaces the sea of Sicily;
    And her who with a quill in her right hand
Writes as one overwhelmed with desperate grief,
And in her left hand holds the dagger close;
    Pygmalion, with his statue come to life;
And many more whose names had oft been sung
By Helicon and the Castalian spring;
    And fair Cydippe, whom an apple won.

III

    So filled with marvels was this heart of mine
That like a man who cannot speak I stood,
Waiting in silence for another's voice,

Till my friend said to me: "What thinkest thou?
Why dost thou ever gaze? Knowest thou not
That I am of the throng, and must move on?"

"Brother," I answered, "well thou knowest me:
So eagerly do I desire to learn
That the desire itself impedes my learning."

And he: "Thy silence I can comprehend:
Thou dost desire to know these other folk,
And I will tell thee, if it be allowed.

Behold him there to whom the rest pay honor,
For he is Pompey. With him is Cornelia:
Of the vile Ptolemy she complains and weeps.

Beyond him, the great Grecian king sees not
The evil Clytemnestra nor Aegisthus:
Now canst thou tell if love be blind indeed!

See Hypermnestra, faithful in her love;
See Pyramus and Thisbe in the shade,
Leander swimming, Hero at the window.

Ulysses moves in thought, a kindly soul:
His faithful wife entreats him to return,
But ardent Circe will not let him go.

Then comes Hamilcar's son, whom for so long
Nor Rome nor all of Italy could defeat;
Yet he fell captive to an Apulian maid.

She who, with locks shorn closely, everywhere
Follows her lord, in Pontus ruled as queen,
But is herself in servitude to love.

Portia refines her love by fire and steel;
Julia complains that Pompey's love for her
Has faded, yielding to a second flame.

Now look this way: behold the patriarch,
Mocked and yet constant, who through seven years
Served to win Rachel, then for seven more:

A mighty love that hardship could not quell!
Behold his father, and his father's sire,
Who with his wife went out to a new land.

See then how love in evil cruelty
Overcame David, leading him to a sin
He was to weep for in a dark retreat.

See how the cloud of love likewise obscures
The clear fame of the wisest of his sons,
Leading him far astray from the Lord above.

Of another son, who loves and yet loves not,
Tamar, o'erwhelmed by her disdainful grief,
Turns in complaint to her brother Absalom.

Closely beyond her, Samson you may see,
Stronger than he is wise, who foolishly
Laid low his head upon a hostile lap.

There too is Holophernes, overcome
In spite of swords and lances, by the words
And the cheeks of a widow, and by love and sleep.
    And see her then, as with her serving-maid
She bears on her return the dreadful head,
In haste, at midnight, giving thanks to God.
    See Shechem, stained with the doubly flowing blood
Of slaughter and of rite, and with him see
His father and his people caught by fraud—
    All this the outcome of a sudden love.
See how Ahasuerus seeks to cure
His love, that he may find some quietness:
    One knot he severs, and another ties,
Finding a remedy for his distress
E'en as one nail may drive another out.
    If thou wouldst witness in a single heart
Delight and dole, bitter and sweet, behold
Herod, beset by love and cruelty.
    See how he burns, how then he turns to rage:
Repenting him of his own fearsome sin,
He cries for Mariamne, who hears not.
    Here are three ladies fair who loved right well,
Procris and Artemisia, and with them
Deidamia. Here are other three

Whose love was evil: and Semiramis,
Byblis and Myrrha are oppressed with shame
For their unlawful and distorted love.

　　Here too are those who fill our books with dreams:
Lancelot, Tristram, and the other knights
Whose wand'rings lead the common folk astray;

　　Guinevere and Iseult, among the rest;
The twain of Rimini, who together go,
Forever uttering their sad laments."

　　Thus did he speak; and I, as one who dreads
A coming ill, and trembles ere he hears
The sound of the trumpet, and feels future wounds,

　　Was pale as one removèd from the tomb,
When by my side appeared a youthful maid,
Purer by far than e'en the whitest dove.

　　She took me captive: I, who would have sworn
To make defense against men bearing arms,
Was bounden by her words and by her ways.

　　And as I now remember, then my friend
Came closer to me, and he laughed at me—
Thinking thereby to give me greater dole—

　　And whispered to me: "Now thou too art free
Thyself to speak to any of us all,
For all of us are stained with the same pitch."

I was as one of those who more regret
Another's good than one's own ill, seeing her,
My capturer, in liberty and peace.

And as I know too well, and all too late,
Her beauty wrought a deadly snare for me,
Burning with envy, jealousy, and love.

I could not take my eyes from her fair face—
As one who is ill, and yet desires a food
Sweet to the taste, but certain to do harm—

To every other pleasure blind and deaf,
Following her through paths so perilous
That I still tremble when I think of them.

Since then mine eyes have been downcast and wet,
My heart oppressed with care, my shelter nought
Save founts and streams, and mountains, woods, and rocks.

Ever since then the pages that I fill
With thoughts and tears and ink are soon destroyed,
And others written for no better fate.

Ever since then I know the life of love,
By love imprisoned, with love's hopes and fears
Writ on my brow for him who will to read.

The fair one whom I hunt eludes me still,
Careless of me and of my sufferings,
Proud of her power and my captivity.

And yet, if I discern aright, this lord,
The lord of love, who dominates the world,
Fears her, and leaves me thus bereft of hope.

I have no strength or courage for defense:
He in whom I had hoped still leads her on
In cruelty to others and to me.

No one can bind her with the bonds of love:
Rebellious and untamed she goes her way
Alone, love's banners meaning nought to her.

A bearing that is hers and only hers,
Her smile, her words, and even her disdains
Make her, in truth, a sun among the stars.

Her locks, now bound in gold, now free to the wind,
Her eyes, illumined with celestial light,
Inflame me, making me content to burn.

Who could find words to tell of what she is,
Of her benignity and gentlehood?
My words are but as brooks are to the sea.

No one like her has e'er been seen before
Nor yet will ever be beheld again,
No tongue can say of her what should be said.

Thus I am captive, and thus she is free.
I entreat day and night (O evil star!),
And of a thousand prayers she scarce hears one.

Hard is the law of Love! but though unjust
One must obey it, for that law prevails
Throughout the universe, and lasts for aye.

Now know I how the heart is rent in twain,
And how it can make peace or war or truce,
And how it may conceal its malady,

And how my blood retreats, and leaves me pale
When I am filled with fear, or rushes red
Into my cheeks, when I am stirred by shame.

I know the serpent hiding in the grass,
And how uncertainty may banish sleep,
How without illness one may faint and die.

I know the seeking of my lady's ways,
And fear of finding her; and I know how
I am transformèd into her I love.

I know the changing of my mood and will
And color, 'mid long sighs and brief delight,
My very soul divided from my heart.

I can deceive myself a thousand times
Within a day; and, following her, I freeze
When I am near her, burning when afar.

I know how Love can roar throughout the mind,
Expelling thought; and in how many ways
The heart may suffer till it faint and fail.

I know how little hemp it takes to bind
A gentle soul, when it is all alone
And there is none to help in its defense.

I know how Love may fly and bend his bow,
How now he threatens, and how now he strikes,
And how he steals and bears his theft away.

I know how mutable his actions are,
How arm'd his hands, how blinded are his eyes,
His promises how empty of all faith,

And how his fire feeds still upon my frame
And lives, a hidden passion, in my veins,
Burning me evermore, and threatening death:

A little sweetness ends in bitterness.

IV

After my fortune into another's power
Had driven me, and had cut all the nerves
Of the liberty that erstwhile had been mine,

I, who had been as wild as the forest deer,
Was swiftly tamed, even as all the rest
Of those who suffered in Love's servitude.

Their toils I witnessed, and the fruits of toil,
And saw what tortuous ways and what deceits
Had made them captives in the train of Love.

While I was looking here and there to see
If any of them had risen to renown
For pages they had writ, or old or new,
    I beheld him who loved Eurydice:
E'en to the world below he followed her,
And calls her still, with a tongue now cold in death.
    I saw Alcaeus, skilled in verse of love,
And Pindar, and Anacreon, who led
His Muses into the one port of Love;
    And I saw Virgil; and it seemed to me
He had companions whom the olden world
Had gladly read, for wisdom and delight:
    Ovid was there, and with him were Catullus,
Propertius, and Tibullus, and they all
Were fervid singers of the power of Love.
    And with these noble poets, side by side,
Singing, there went a gentle Grecian maid,
Whose manner was her own, and sweet and rare.
    And looking then now this way and now that,
I saw folk coming over a green sward,
Speaking of love, but in the common tongue:
    Dante and Beatrice, Cino and her he loved,
Guittone of Arezzo, ill content
Not to be held as first among them all.

Here were both Guidos, held in high esteem;
And Ser Onesto; and from Sicily
Those who, once first, were now no more than last;
    Sennuccio and Franceschino, kindly men,
As all men knew. Then came a company
Foreign in dress, and foreign in their speech:
    First of them all was Arnaut Daniel,
Master in love; and he his native land
Honors with the strange beauty of his verse.

    Here too were ready prisoners of Love,
Both Peires, and the less far-famed Arnaut;
And those whom Love found harder to defeat:
    The two Raimbauts, one of them he who sang
Of Monferrato and its Beatrice;
And the old Peire d'Alvernhe, and Giraut;
    Folquet, who to Marseilles has given the name
He took from Genoa, and at the end of life
Changed dress and state to win a better land;
    Jaufre Rudel, who used both sail and oar
In voyaging to his death; and that Guillem
Who for his singing lost the flower of life.
    Aimeric and Bernart, Uc and Gaucelm,
And many more I saw, for whom the tongue
Was ever lance and sword, helmet and targe.

I turned again—since I must voice my grief—
To our own folk, and saw Tomasso there,
Ornament of Bologna, who lies now

 In a Sicilian grave. Oh sweetness brief,
Oh weary life! Who carried thee away
So soon, thou who wast ever by my side?

 Where art thou now, who lately wast with me?
This mortal life, that we do cherish so,
Is an ill dream, a tale of vain romance!

 Not far from the common path had I yet moved
When first I saw my Socrates, and with him
My Laelius: with them I still move on.

 Oh what a pair of friends! Never could I
In verse or prose tell rightly of their worth
If at its due pure virtue be esteemed.

 With these twain I have traveled many lands,
A common yoke holding us close together:
To them I told the tale of all my wounds.

 Nor time nor distance e'er shall separate
Us from each other—so I hope and pray—
Until for us the funeral pyres be lit.

 With them I plucked the glorious laurel branch
Wherewith—perhaps too soon—I decked my brow,
Remembering her whom I so deeply love.

And yet from her, who fills my heart with thoughts,
Ne'er have I gathered either branch or leaf,
So hard and so unyielding were her roots.

Wherefore, though overcome with grief betimes,
Like one offended, what I now beheld
With mine own eyes bids me to grieve no more.

Matter for tragedy, not for comedy,
To see him captured who is held a god
By slow and blunted and deluded minds!

But first I'll tell of what he did with us
And then of all that he himself endured—
A tale for Homer, or for Orpheus!

We followed, in the sound of the red wings
Of the flying coursers, through a thousand woes,
Until to his maternal realm he came;

Nor were our chains made lighter or removed
As we were drawn through mountain heights and woods,
So that we knew not in what world we were.

Beyond the Aegean's sighs and tears there lies
The softest and the gentlest of all isles
Warmed by the sun or watered by the sea;

And hidden in the midst a shadowy hill
With fragrances so sweet and streams so clear
That from the heart they banish manly thoughts.

31

This is the land that Venus held so dear—
Sacred to her it was in the olden time
When truth lay still unknown and unrevealed—
    And even now it is so reft of worth,
Holds still so much of its first pagandom,
That to the bad 'tis sweet, sour to the good.
    Here then to triumph came the mighty lord
Of us and all whom with the selfsame snare
He had caught, from Thule to the Indian sea:
    Thoughts in our bosoms, emptiness to grasp,
Fleeting delights, and constant weariness,
Roses in winter, ice in summertime;
    Before us doubtful love and fleeting joy,
Behind us nought but penitence and dole—
As the realm of Rome well knows, and that of Troy;
    And the whole valley echoed with the songs
Of waters and of birds, and all its swards
Were white and green and red and yellow and perse.
    Streamlets that spring from living fountains run
Through the fresh verdure in the summer heat
When shade is deep and gentle is the breeze:
    And then, when winter comes and the air is cool,
Warm sun, games, food, and torpid idleness
That casts its evil spell on foolish hearts.

It was the season when the equinox
Gives victory to the day, and Procne comes,
And Philomel, for their sweet springtime task.

Alas, the instability of fate!
For there, and at the very time and hour
That draws a tearful tribute from my eyes

He held his triumph whom the common folk
Adore, and I beheld what servitude
And death and torment wait for one who loves.

Errors and dreams and vain imaginings
Were gathered at his great triumphal arch,
And at his palace gates were false beliefs,

And slippery hopes were high upon the stairs
Where he who climbs the highest falls the most,
Where it is ill to gain and well to lose;

Weary repose, peace hardly to be won,
Dishonor bright, and glory dark and black,
Perfidious loyalty and constant fraud;

Incessant madness, slothfulness in thought,
A prison entered by wide-open gates
Whence passage for escape is ill to find;

Descending slopes that are of steep ascent.
Within the palace mad confusion reigns
Of certain sorrows and uncertain joys.

Ne'er boiled volcano with such furious rage—
Lipari, Ischia, Aetna, Stromboli.
Who risks such game has little thought for self.
 It was within this dark and narrow cage
That we were shut, and there, and all too soon
My hair turned white, and all my looks were changed;
 And all the while, dreaming of liberty,
I fed my soul, impatient for escape,
By thinking of the loves of olden times.
 Like snow that melts away in the sun was I,
Gazing at the great spirits here confined—
Like one beholding lengthy painted scenes,
 Whose eyes look back, despite his hurried feet.

THE TRIUMPH OF CHASTITY

WHEN AT one time and under one same yoke
I saw the pride of gods Olympian
So tamed, and that of men almost divine,

    I took example from their sorry state,
Deriving from the sight of their distress
Some consolation for my fated woes.

    For if two arrows from a single bow
Can wound Apollo and the young Leander,
One called a god, the other but a man,

    And if in a single snare Juno may fall,
And Dido, she whom love for her own spouse
(Not—as they say—for Aeneas) drove to her death,

    I should not grieve if I be overcome,
Being young, unarmed, incautious, and alone.
And if Love conquered not mine enemy

    Not even that is cause enough for grief:
For in such plight that I could weep for him
I saw him soon, captive and reft of his wings.

As when two lions roaring in their rage
Together crash, or blazing thunderbolts
Plunge downward, riving air and earth and sea,

    So I saw Love, with all his armaments,
Moving to capture her of whom I write,
Swifter than flame or wind in her defense.

    And far more terrible than the mighty sounds
Of Aetna shaken by Enceladus,
Or Scylla and Charybdis in their wrath,

    Was the first clash of the two combatants—
The outcome of the dread assault unsure—
Nor have I words to tell of it aright.

    All of the captives, then, with one accord,
Withdrew to a high place, to witness thence
A battle that turned hearts and eyes to stone.

    That conqueror, moving first to the attack,
Held in his hands an arrow and a bow,
The bowstring drawn already to his ear.

    So swiftly did Love move to strike her down
Who bears in her face the eyes that kindle me,
That e'en a leopard, practiced in the hunt

    Or free to roam in the forest, would have been
Less swift in hasting to an open place
Where he might leap upon a fleeing deer.

Pity contended in me with desire,
For she to me would be a sweet companion,
Yet 'twould be hard to see her overcome.

    Virtue, that never doth forsake the good,
Proved then how deeply in the wrong is he
Who, leaving her, complains of his defeat.

    Never was there a fencer so adept
At turning blows aside, never a pilot
So quick to save a ship from harbor rocks,

    As she, her lovely face at once o'erspread
With valor and honor, was to fend the blow
That, if awaited, brings fatality.

    I watched to the end, with eyes and heart intent,
Hoping that Love would win, as was his wont,
And I no more be held apart from her;

    And like to one compelled by great desire
Whose words, before he even starts to speak,
Are written in his eyes and on his brow

    I would have said: "My lord, if thou dost win
Bind me with her, if I thereof be worthy,
And have no fear that I shall seek release" —

    When I beheld him filled with wrath so fierce
Not e'en the greatest pens could tell of it,
Much less the little skill that is in me.

For now his gilded shafts, lit with the flame
Of amorous beauty, and in pleasure dipped,
Were by the coldness of her honor quenched.

Camilla's valor was no more than a dram,
And that of her companion Amazons,
Who sacrificed a breast for archery,

Nor in Pharsalia, 'gainst his daughter's spouse,
Did Caesar strive so ardently as she
'Gainst him who shatters every coat of mail.

With her, and armèd, was the glorious host
Of all the radiant virtues that were hers,
Hands held in hands that clasped them, two by two.

Honor and Modesty were in the van,
A noble pair of virtues excellent,
That set her high above all other women;

Prudence and Moderation were near by,
Benignity and Gladness of the Heart—
Glory and Perseverance in the rear;

Foresight and Graciousness were at the sides,
And Courtesy therewith, and Purity,
Desire for Honor, and the Fear of Shame.

A Thoughtfulness mature in spite of Youth,
And, in a concord rarely to be found,
Beauty supreme at one with Chastity.

So moved she against Love, and favored so
By heaven, and such a host of well-born souls,
That he could not withstand the massive sight.

    Thousands of victims, famed and dear, from him
She rescued; and a thousand shining palms
Of victory she wrested from his hands.

    Nor was the sudden fall of Hannibal,
After so many victories, so strange,
When he was vanquished by the Roman youth;

    Nor in the vale of Terebinth so dazed
Lay the Philistine giant from whose might
All Israel had fled, when he was struck

    By the first stone slung by the Hebrew boy;
Nor Cyrus when the widowed Scythian queen
Wrought fearful vengeance for her slaughtered son.

    Like one who, being well, falls suddenly ill,
And is afraid and troubled, or is caught
In an act so shameful that he hides his eyes,

    So now was Love, but in still worse a plight,
Since fear and grief and shame and wrathfulness
Were all together written on his face:

    Greater his rage than that of the angry sea,
Or that of Ischia when Typhoeus weeps,
Or Aetna's when Enceladus laments.

I leave untold things glorious and great
That I beheld and dare not tell: I come
Now to my lady and her lesser friends.
  She wore, that day, a gown of white, and held
The shield that brought Medusa to her death.
To a fair jasper column that was there,
  And with a chain once dipped in Lethe's stream—
A chain of diamond and topaz, such
As women used to wear, but wear no more—
  I saw him bound, and saw him then chastised
Enough to wreak a thousand vengeances:
And I was well content, and satisfied.
  I could not fairly celebrate in rhyme,
Nor could Calliope and the Muses all,
The host of holy women who were there;
  But I will tell of some in the forefront
Of truest honor; and among them all
Lucretia and Penelope were first,
  For they had broken all the shafts of Love
And torn away the quiver from his side,
And they had plucked the feathers from his wings.
  Then came Virginia, and her father arm'd
With sword and with affection and with wrath,
Who changed her state and changed the state of Rome:

44

For one and the other did he now set free.
Then came the German women who chose death
Their own barbaric honor to preserve;

The Hebrew Judith, wise and chaste and strong;
And the Greek maid who plunged into the sea
To flee an evil fate, and die unstained.

With these and other souls illustrious
I saw my lady triumph over him
I had seen triumph over all the world.

Among the others was the vestal maid
Who that she might be free of ill report
Sped boldly to the Tiber, and from thence

Brought water to her temple in a sieve.
Then came the Sabines and Hersilia,
A troop whose honored fame fills many a tome.

And there I saw, 'mid those of other lands,
Her who for a belov'd and faithful spouse
(Not for Aeneas) willed to meet her end.

Let ignorance be still! I speak of her,
Dido, whom honor led to death, and not
An empty love, as is the public cry.

And I saw one who where the Arno flows
Renounced the world; yet it availed her not:
Another's force o'ercame her good intent.

The triumph now had come, in the warmth of Spring,
To Baia's shore, where beat the salty waves,
And landed there, and turned to the right hand.

Thence, passing by the Sybil's ancient cave,
'Twixt Monte Barbaro and the Avernian Lake
Straight to Linterno was its onward course.

There in his simple home, living in peace
Was the great Africanus, titled thus
Since 'twas his sword that opened Africa;

And here the tidings of the victory,
Not lessened by beholding, gave delight:
Fairest of all was she who was most chaste.

And he to join a triumph not his own
Was ready, who—as is believed of him—
Was born for triumphs and imperial might.

Unto the sovereign city thus we came,
First to the temple that Sulpicia built
To quench the flame of madness in the mind,

And then at last to the fane of Chastity,
That kindles pure desires within the heart,
Fit for patrician, not plebeian, folk.

There the fair victress spread her glorious spoils
And there she left the crown that she had won,
The sacred laurel crown of victory.

And there to guard the common foe she set
The Tuscan youth who in his face displayed
The wounds that made him not a cause for fear,
    With several others (and the names of some
Were told me by my guide, who knew them all),
And these were youths who had dared to challenge Love:
    Among them Joseph and Hippolytus.

THE TRIUMPH OF DEATH

I

THAT LADY, glorious and beautiful,
Who, once a pillar of high excellence,
Is now but spirit and a little earth,

    In honor was returning from her war,
Glad for her victory over the great foe
Who with his fraudulence afflicts the world—

    Her weapons none save purity of heart,
Beauty of countenance and modest thought,
And converse ever virtuous and wise.

    And it was wondrous in her train to see,
Shattered, the arrows and the bow of Love,
And those whom he had captured or had slain.

    Returning from their noble victory
The lovely lady with a chosen few
Together made a troop that was but small—

    The glory that is true is ever rare—
But for herself each one of them deserved
A noble poem, or historic fame.

The banner of their victory displayed
An ermine white upon a field of green,
Wearing a chain of topaz and of gold.

Not human, rather to be called divine,
Were both their bearing and their holy words:
Blessèd is one born for such destiny!

With violets and roses they were decked;
Bright stars they seemed, and in their midst a sun
Adorned them all, and made them brighter still.

And as a gentle heart wins honor, so
The troop was moving onward joyously,
When I beheld a banner dark and sad,

And a woman shrouded in a dress of black,
With fury such as had perchance been seen
When giants raged in the Phlegraean vale,

Came near, and said: "O thou who goest on,
Proud of thy beauty and thy youthfulness,
And know'st not when thy life shall reach its end,

I am that one whom all ye mortals call
Fierce and relentless: ye are deaf and blind,
Night falls upon you ere 'tis eventide.

'Twas I who brought the Grecians to their fate,
And Troy, and then the Romans last of all,
With this my sword, that cuts and plunges deep,

And other peoples, barbarous and strange;
And coming when there is least heed of me,
I put an end to infinite vain thoughts.

And now to you, when life delights you most,
I take my course, ere Fortune strike at you,
Turning your sweetness into bitterness."

"Thou hast no power over those with me" —
Thus answered she who was without a peer —
"And little over me, save for my body.

I know that there is one who more than I
Will grieve, who needeth me for his soul's sake;
But I shall grateful be for my release."

As one who bends her eyes on something strange,
Perceiving what before she had not seen,
Marveling and regretful for her error,

Such now was this dread creature: but ere long
"Well do I recognize them all," she said,
"And know when they were bitten by my tooth."

Then, with her brow less troubled and less dark
She said: "Thou who dost lead this goodly throng,
And yet hast never felt my poisonous touch,

If thou hast any trust in what I say,
Who can enforce my will, 'tis better far
To shun old age and all its many woes.

I am disposed to honor thee in a way
Unwonted, and to let thee pass from life
Free from all fear and from all suffering."

"As it may please the Lord who is in heaven
And rules and moderates the universe,
Do with me as thou dost with all mankind."

'Twas thus she answered; and then suddenly
The vale was filled with folk already dead,
Beyond the power of prose or verse to tell.

The plain itself and all its slopes were filled
With a great host of the dead of many times,
From India, Cathay, Morocco, Spain.

Here now were they who were called fortunate,
Popes, emperors, and others who had ruled;
Now are they naked, poor, of all bereft.

Where now their riches? Where their honors now?
Where now their gems and scepters, and their crowns,
Their miters, and the purple they had worn?

Wretched who sets his hope on mortal things—
Yet who does not?—and if he find himself
Deluded at the last, it is but just.

What profit have ye from your blind pursuits?
Ye all return to the great ancient mother:
Even the memory of your names is lost.

Of your unnumbered tasks is there e'en one
That is aught more than merest vanity?
Let him reply who knows what ye have done.
    Avails it aught to conquer other lands
And make their foreign people tributary,
Your will enkindled ever for their harm?
    After emprises perilous and vain
And lands and treasures won with your own blood,
Ye will find bread and water far more sweet,
    And wood and glass better than gems and gold.
But, following no more so long a theme,
'Tis time that I return to my prime task.
    So I declare that for her earthly life,
Brief and renown'd, the final hour had come,
And the doubtful passing that the world doth dread.
    There to behold her was another throng
Of worthy women still in life, who came
To see if it may be that Death be kind.
    This noble company was gathered there
To see and contemplate the fatal end
That comes to all of us, and comes but once:
    They were her friends and neighbors, every one.
And then from her blond head the hand of Death
Plucked forth a single sacred golden strand;

And thus she chose the whole world's fairest flower,
Not out of hatred, but to demonstrate
Her sovereignty o'er e'en the highest things.

Weeping and sad laments abounded there,
And only those fair eyes of hers were dry
For which I sang and burned so many years.

Amid the sighing and the sorrowing
Silent and well content she sat alone,
Gathering now the fruit of her good life.

"Go then in peace," they said, "O thou who art
A mortal goddess." Such she was, and yet
Naught could prevail 'gainst Death's relentless power.

Night after night she had suffered burning pain,
Now less, now more: how then shall others fare?
O human hopes! how blind and false ye are!

If many tears fell then upon the earth,
Called forth by pity for her gentle soul,
Who saw them, knows: thou, listener, mayst but think.

April the sixth, it was, and the first hour,
When I was bound—and now, alas, set free!
Surely the ways of fate are strange indeed!

None ever grieved so much for servitude,
Even for death, as I for liberty,
And that my life was not now ta'en from me.

'Twas due this age of ours, and due the world,
That I, who first had come, should first have gone,
And that its brightest honor should remain.

Grief beyond measure filled us all: I scarce
Dare think of it, and even less be bold
Enough to speak thereof in verse or rhyme.

"Virtue is dead, beauty and gentleness"—
'Twas thus by her chaste bed the ladies all
Spoke sadly: "What shall now become of us?

Who now will see her perfect way of life?
Who now will hear the wisdom of her words,
Or the angelic sweetness of her song?"

Her spirit, ready now to leave her breast,
Was gathering her virtues to itself,
And the heaven above her had become serene.

No evil adversary ventured then
To make appearance with malignant mien
Before the task of Death was all complete.

And now, the time for fear and weeping past,
All were intent upon her lovely face,
Despair bringing to them its certainty.

Not like a flame that forcibly is quenched,
But like to one that doth itself consume,
Her soul, contented, went its way in peace,

Like to a light that is both clear and sweet
And loses slowly its own nutriment,
Keeping its dearness to the very end.

　　Not pale, but whiter than the whitest snow
Quietly falling on a gentle hill,
She seemed to be aweary and at rest.

　　And that which is called "death" by foolish folk
Was a sweet sleep upon her lovely eyes,
Now that her body held her soul no more;

　　And even death seemed fair in her fair face.

II

　　The night that followed the dread stroke of fate
That quenched the sun—nay, lifted it to heaven,
Leaving me lost and blind upon the earth—

　　Was spreading through the air the coolness sweet
That with the whiteness of Tithonus' mate
Is wont to take the veil from dreams confused,

　　When toward me, from among a thousand crowns,
There came a lady like unto the Spring,
Crowned with a diadem of orient gems.

　　Speaking and sighing, she held out to me—
Bringing eternal sweetness to my heart—
The hand that I so greatly had desired.

"Knowest thou her who first, and long ago,
Guided thy steps away from the common path?"
Pensive she was, and humble, and yet wise,

    As when my heart was first aware of her.
She sat, and I beside her, by a stream
O'ershaded by a laurel and a beech.

    "How could I fail to know my heavenly guide?"
I answered, like to one who speaks and weeps,
"Tell me, I pray, art thou in life or death?"

    "I am in life, and thou art still in death,"
She said, "as thou wilt be until there come
The hour that shall release thee from the earth.

    Our time is short, and our desire is long:
Therefore take thought, and count and check thy words
Ere we be parted by the light of day."

    And I: "When earthly life comes to its end,
Pray tell me, thou who knowest it by proof,
If death be fraught with bitter suffering."

    She answered: "Following the common herd
In all the blindness of their stubborn thought,
Never canst thou attain to happiness.

    Death is the end of dark imprisonment
For gentle souls, but bringeth agony
To those whose cares rise not above the mire;

And mine own death, that causeth thee such grief,
Would bring thee gladness, if thou couldst but know
A thousandth part of the joy that now is mine."

Thus did she speak, her eyes devoutly raised
To heaven; then in silence did she move
Her rosy lips, until I spoke again:

"Mezentius, Sulla, Nero, Marius,
Gaius, and burning fevers and racking pains,
Make wormwood seem less bitter than death's sting."

"The failing of the breath before the end,"
Thus she replied, "is hard indeed to bear,
And harder still the fear of lasting woe;

But if the soul hath placed its trust in God
And the heart also, weary though it be,
What more is death than a mere moment's sigh?

When I was near the hour of my passing,
My spirit willing, though my flesh was weak,
I heard a sorrowing voice say quietly:

'Oh sad indeed is he who counts the days,
Each one a thousand years to him. In vain
He lives, no more to meet her on this earth.

He seeks the sea, and travels all its shores,
And yet no wandering brings change to him:
Of her alone he thinks and speaks and writes.'

Then to the place whence came these words to me
I turned my weary eyes, and saw her there
Who, for us both, urged me, restraining thee.

I recognized her by her face and speech,
Who often had brought comfort to my heart:
Now grave and wise, and ever true and fair.

When I was in my fairest earthly state
In glowing youth, and unto thee most dear—
Whence many have found cause to think and speak—

My life was hardly less than bitter, then,
Compared to the sweet kindliness of death
Vouchsafed to me—and rarely to mankind.

In all my passing I was more content,
Than one from exile coming to a dear home,
Save for the pity that I felt for thee."

"Prithee, Madonna, by the faithfulness
That while you lived was manifest to you
And in the sight of God is now confirmed,

Did ever love create within your mind
The thought of taking pity on my plight,
Within the bounds your sense of honor set?

Your sweet reproaches and your sweet disdains
And the sweet signs of peace in your fair eyes
Kept my desire in doubt for many years."

Scarce had I said these words when I beheld
The flashing of that smile so sweet to me,
That once had been a sun to cheer my spirit.

    Sighing, she answered: "Never was my heart
From thee divided, nor shall ever be.
Thy flame I tempered with my countenance

    Because there was no other way than this
To save us both, and save your youthful fame:
A mother loves, even with lash in hand.

    How often to myself I said: 'He loves,
Nay more, he burns, and is in need of help,
Scarce to be had from one who hopes and fears:

    Let him behold my face, and not my heart.'
And this it was that often turned thee back
And checked thee, as a frightened steed is checked.

    More than a thousand times anger appeared
Upon my face, while love glowed in my heart,
But reason ever conquered my desire.

    And when I saw thee overcome with grief
I looked upon thee then with kindly eyes,
Safeguarding thus our honor and thy life;

    And if thy suffering were too intense
Making me sorrowful or timorous,
My brow and voice more gently greeted thee.

These my devices were, and these my arts,
Now benign welcoming, and now disdain—
Thou knowest, who hast often sung thereof.

    For there were times when I beheld thine eyes
So tearful that I thought: 'I see the signs,
He is undone, unless some help be given'—

    And then as best I could I succored thee.
At other times I saw thee so aflame
I said: 'Now needeth he a tighter bit.'

    And thus, now warm and red, now cold and white,
Now sad, now glad, I have conducted thee
Safe (and therefor do I rejoice), but weary."

    Then trembling, and with tears upon my face,
I said: "Madonna, great reward were this
For all my faith, if I could but believe."

    "Of little faith! for if I knew it not,
Or knew not it was true, why should I tell?"
She answered, and her face seemed flushed to me.

    "Whether thou didst bring pleasure to my eyes
I will not say; but pleasure that sweet knot
Did give me that thou hadst around thy heart,

    And pleasure the fair name thy poetry
Hath won for me, I ween, both near and far.
All that I sought was measure in thy love:

I never found it. While in sorrowful guise
Thou wouldst have shown me what I always saw,
Thou didst reveal thy heart to all the world.

Thence came the coolness that still troubles thee,
For in all else we were as much at one
As love comports, within the bounds of honor.

The flames of love burned almost equally
In us, after I knew the fire in thee:
But one of us revealed them, one did not.

Thou wast already hoarse, calling for mercy,
While I was silent, since my fear and shame
Combined to make my great desire seem small.

Dole that is hidden is no less a pain,
Nor is it made the larger by laments,
For no pretense greatens or lessens truth.

But was not every veil between us rent
When in thy presence I received thy verse,
And sang, 'Our love dares not say more than this'?

My heart was thine, but I controlled mine eyes.
For this thou grievest, thinking I was wrong:
What I withheld was least, what I gave, best.

Knowest thou not that though mine eyes were turned
Away from thee a thousand times and more,
They were restored, and looked on thee with pity?

And peacefully would I have let them turn
Ever to thee, had I not been afraid
Of the parlous flames that shone within thine eyes.

Now that the time of parting is so near
I will say more, to leave thee not without
A final word that thou mayst cherish still.

Though I was richly blest in other ways,
In one sole matter was I ill content:
That I was born in such a lowly place.

Regretful am I that I was not born
Nearer, at least, to thine own flowered nest;
But if I pleased thee, coming thence, 'tis well.

For had I been unknown to thee, thy heart,
Wherein I trust, might not have turned to me,
And less renown and fame would have been mine."

"Not so," I answered; "the third heavenly sphere
Unmoved and stable, destined me for a love
As great as this, where'er we might have dwelt."

"So be it then," she said, "for honor comes
To me, and still is mine. But in thy joy
Thou countest not the passing of the hours.

See how Aurora from her golden bed
Brings the day back to mortals, while the sun
Is lifting now his breast above the sea:

She came to part us, and therefor I grieve.
If thou hast more to say, seek to be brief,
Remembering how short a time remains."

"Your kind and loving words have made it seem
That all my sufferings were light and sweet,
But life without you will be hard for me.

Therefore, Madonna, this I fain would know:
Shall it be soon or late that I follow you?"
And she, departing, said: " 'Tis my belief

Thou wilt be long without me on the earth."

THE TRIUMPH OF FAME

I

WHEN DEATH had triumphed in the countenance
That had so often triumphed over me,
And when the sun was taken from our world,

   That pitiless and evil one had gone,
Pallid in aspect, horrible, and proud,
By whom the light of beauty had been quenched.

   Then, as I gazed across the grassy vale
I saw appearing on the other side
Her who saves man from the tomb, and gives him life.

   As at the break of day an amorous star
Comes from the east before the rising sun,
Who gladly enters her companionship,

   Thus came she. From what rhetoricians' school
Shall come the master who could fully tell
What I shall only tell in simple words?

   The sky all round about was now so bright
My eyes were vanquished by its brilliancy,
In spite of the desire that filled my heart.

Those who attended her bore on their brows
The signs of worthiness: among them were
Some I had seen aforetime bound by Love.

At her right hand, where first I bent mine eyes,
Were Scipio and Caesar; but which one
Was closer to her I could not discern.

One of the twain served virtue and not love,
The other served them both. Then there appeared,
Following those who were so glorious,

Folk armed alike with valor and with steel,
As in the triumphs that in olden times
Proceeded through the sacred ways of Rome.

They came in the order I shall now set forth,
And every one in aspect seemed to bear
The name that is most glorious of all.

I was intent upon their noble talk,
Their faces, and their actions. The first two
Were followed by a grandson, and a son

Who was unique and peerless in the world;
And those who willed to block the enemy
With their own bodies, fathers two, were there,

Companioned by three sons. One went before,
And two came afterward: the last being first
In honor for the praise that he had won.

Then, flashing like a ruby bright, came one
Who with his counsel and his bravery
Rescued all Italy in the time of need:

I speak of Claudius, who in the silent night,
When he saw the Metaurus, came to purge
The fields of Rome of all their evil growth,

For he had eyes for sight, and wings for speed.
And after him there came a great old man
Who with his art held Hannibal at bay.

With him, two Catos and two Fabii,
Two Pauli, Bruti two, and two Marcelli,
Regulus, who loved others more than self;

Curio and Fabricius, nobler far
In poverty than Midas with his gold,
Or Crassus, rebels against honesty;

Serranus following ever in their steps,
With Cincinnatus; great Camillus then,
Weary of life, but not of serving Rome;

For he so highly won the honor of heaven
That his clear virtue led him to return
Thither whence a blind rage had driven him.

Then came Torquatus, he who smote his son,
Preferring to be reft of him than that
His troops be reft of spirit and of strength;

Then the two Decii who with their breasts
Opened the hostile ranks. Oh fearsome vow,
That offered father and son to one same death!

    With them came Curtius, like to them avowed,
Who plunged in armor into the great cave
That horribly within the Forum yawned;

    Laevinus, Mummius, and Attilius;
Flaminius, who conquered Greece by force,
But even more by generosity.

    He too was there who drew a noble ring
Around the Syrian king, and with his brow
And with his tongue compelled him to consent;

    And he who, arm'd, alone, defended once
A hill whence later he was hurled; and he
Who held a bridge against all Tuscany;

    He also who had raised his hand in vain
Amid the enemy's host, and burned it then,
So wrathful that he felt no pain therefrom;

    And he who first was victor on the sea
Against the Carthaginians; and he
Who by the islands scattered all their fleet;

    Appius, blinded, and his kindred all,
Ever oppressive to the humble plebs.
Then saw I a great man of gentle mien,

Who had been first had not his light grown dim:
He surely was for us as were for Thebes
Epaminondas, Bacchus, and Hercules.

But it is ill to live too long! And next
Him I beheld, the flower of his time,
Who from his skill and swiftness had his name.

He in command was cruel and severe;
But he who followed was of kindly heart,
Worthy as captain and as man-at-arms.

Noble Volumnius, meriting high praise,
Came then, who by his conduct had removed
A bleeding tumor, livid, and malign;

Cossus and Philo and Rutilius;
Then, at one side, three by themselves I saw,
Their bodies wounded, and their armor cleft,

Three thunderbolts and mighty cliffs of war,
Dentatus, Scaeva, Marcus Sergius,
Who through a younger kinsman lost his fame.

Marius then, who crushed the German rage,
Jugurtha, and the Cimbri; Fulvius,
Who against orders put ingrates to death;

The nobler Fulvius; of the Gracchi one
From all that garrulous and restless brood
That tried the patience of the men of Rome;

Metellus, who to all seemed glad and blest—
I do not say he was, for one sees not
Into a heart shut close in secrecy;
    His father and his heirs were there as well:
From Macedon and from Numidia
They brought their booty, and from Crete and Spain.
    And then I saw Vespasian and the son
Who was fair and good (the other, fair and vile),
Nerva and Trajan, trusty princes both,
    Hadrian, Antonine his foster son,
Marcus Aurelius too—a goodly set,
For good men want good men to follow them.
    While in my eagerness I looked ahead
I saw the founder of Rome and its next five kings:
The last was buried under his burden of shame,
    As doth befall scorners of righteousness.

II

    Filled with amazement endless and profound
At the sight of these heroic men of Rome—
Ne'er in the world was such another host—
    I turned to records of the olden age
Wherein great names and virtues are inscribed,
And found that much was lacking to my tale.

78

Yet now my thoughts to foreign heroes turned:
To Hannibal, and then to Achilles, sung
In verse that gave to him immense renown;

Two famous Trojans; two great Persian kings;
Then Philip, and his son, whose swift campaigns
Won victories from Greece to India;

The other Alexander, near at hand,
Moving less swiftly: he had mightier foes
(How much true honor Fortune tears away!);

The three of Thebes, already named, together;
Then he who sought to see too much of the world,
Ulysses; with him Ajax and Diomed;

Nestor, who knew so much and lived so long;
And Agamemnon, who with Menelaus,
Unhappy in wedlock, filled the world with strife;

Leonidas, who to his troop proposed
A dinner hard, and supper with the dead,
And in a narrow pass wrought wondrously;

And Alcibiades, who so many times
Turned Athens back and forth, to suit his will,
By his fair face and by his honeyed words;

Miltiades, who took the yoke from Greece,
With his good son, who, loving perfectly,
Binding himself, set his dead father free;

Themistocles and Theseus with this group,
And Aristides—like to our Fabricius—
To whom Athenian burial was denied,

   Their excellence illumined by the vice
Of others: nought so well contrasts two acts
As brevity of intervening time;

   Phocion, banished even in his death,
Was of the company of these three men—
Far different from his deeds was his reward!

   Turning mine eyes, I saw the valiant Pyrrhus,
And the good king Masinissa—ill content
That he had not had place in the Roman host.

   Gazing this way and that, I saw with him
The Syracusan Hiero, and then
Cruel Hamilcar, far removed from them.

   The Lydian king I saw, as from the fire
Naked he came, making it manifest
That nought avails against the will of Fate.

   I beheld Syphax, prey to like distress,
Brennus, so many of whose followers fell—
As he too fell, below the Delphic fane.

   Great was the throng, and various in dress.
Then, looking upward toward a height, I saw
A group all closely gathered, and aloof.

Foremost therein was he who planned to build
A dwelling place for God among mankind;
But he who built came after him, for so

    It was ordained. He raised the holy House,
From base to summit—but within his heart
He builded not so well, as I infer.

    Then he who had received such grace from God
That he held converse with Him, face to face,
A privilege no other man can claim;

    And he who, by the virtue of his speech,
Did bind the sun, even as a beast is caught,
That he might still pursue his enemies:

    Oh noble faith! That he who worships God
Is master over all that God creates
And with his simple words may stay the heavens!

    And then I saw our father, who was called
To leave his homeland, and to make his way
To the place that was elect for our salvation;

    With him his son, and his son's son, deceived
As to his wives; and then, somewhat apart,
I saw that son's son, Joseph, wise and chaste;

    And gazing then as far as I could gaze
I saw him beyond whom no eye may reach,
Whose disobedience despoiled the world.

Nearer, I saw the builder of the Ark,
And he who undertook to build the tower
Laden so heavily with fault and sin;
    Then Judas Maccabaeus, who held true
To his father's laws, invincible and bold,
As one rushing on death for a just cause.
    My will to see was growing weary now,
Till I beheld a new and gracious sight
That made me still more eager than before.
    A troop of warrior women now I saw:
Antiope and Orithia, armed and fair;
Hippolyta, mourning for her lifeless son,
    And Menalippe, each of them so swift
That Hercules could hardly vanquish them—
And one he kept, the other gave to Theseus;
    The widow who, unweeping, saw her son
In death, and then for him such vengeance took
That she slew Cyrus, and now slays his fame:
    For even now, hearing his dreadful end,
He seems again to be dying in his guilt,
So much of honor did he lose that day!
    Then I saw her who in an evil hour
Saw Troy; and with them too the Latin maid
Who fought the Trojan band in Italy.

And then I saw the queen, high-spirited,
Who with her hair half kempt and half unkempt
Sped to o'ercome revolt in Babylon,
    And Cleopatra, both of them aflame
With wrongful love; and in the line I saw
Zenobia, more jealous of her honor:
    For she was fair, and in the flower of youth,
And all the more in beauty and in youth
To cherish honor is to merit praise;
    And in her woman's heart was strength so great
That with her beauty and her armored locks
She brought dismay to men unused to fear—
    I speak of the imperial might of Rome
That she assailed in war—albeit at last
She for our triumph was a wealthy prize.
    Among the names that I must disregard
Shall not be that of Judith, widow brave,
Who reft her foolish lover of his head.
    But Ninus, with whom history begins,
Where leave I him? And where his great successor?
Whose pride reduced him to a bestial life?
    Where too is Belus, worshiped sinfully,
But not through his own fault? Where Zoroaster,
With whom the use of magic arts began?

And where is he who, east of the Euphrates,
So fiercely dealt with our ill-starred commanders—
A sorry plaster for Italic woes!

Where the great Mithridates, that eternal
Foe of the Romans—from whose toils he fled,
Summer or winter, to return again!

Much greatness now most briefly I compress.
Where is King Arthur? Where three emperors,
An African, a Spaniard, and a Gaul?

With Arthur were his dozen paladins.
Thereafter the duke Godfrey came alone,
To undertake crusade and righteous steps,

Who in Jerusalem with his own hands
Built the nest now bereft of care or guard,
Whence in my wrath I cry aloud—in vain!

Live on, ye wretched Christians, in your pride,
Consuming one the other, caring not
That the tomb of Christ be in the clutch of dogs!

Few men, if any, saw I after him
Rise to high fame, if I be not deceived,
Either through arts of peace or arts of war.

And yet, as men who are elect come last,
Near to the end I saw the Saracen
Who to our armies brought such shame and harm;

And he of Loria followed Saladin.
Then came the Duke of Lancaster, who erst
Was a rough neighbor to the realm of France.

Then, like a man who presses still ahead,
I strove to see if I could recognize
Any whom I had seen aforetime, here on earth;

And I saw two who only yestereve
Departed from our life and from our land;
They were the two who closed the honored troop:

The good Sicilian king, of high intent,
Truly an Argus in his foresight keen,
And by his side I saw my great Colonna,

Constant and generous, and of noble heart.

III

I scarce could take mine eyes from such a sight
Until a voice said: "Look to the other side:
'Tis not in arms alone that fame is won."

I turned to the left; and Plato there I saw,
Who of them all came closest to the goal
Whereto by Heaven's grace man may attain;

Then Aristotle, of high intellect,
Pythagoras, who in humility
First gave philosophy its fitting name;

Socrates, Xenophon, and the aged bard
To whom the Muses were so kind that Troy
And Argos and Mycenae know thereof:
    He, first to paint men's ancient memories,
Sang of the toils and of the wanderings
Of the son of Laertes, and of a goddess' son.
    And side by side with him, singing, there went
The Mantuan, who seems to rival him,
And one whose passing made the grass to bloom:
    This is that Marcus Tullius, in whom
The fruits and flowers of eloquence appear:
Theirs are the eyes that light our Latin tongue.
    Then came Demosthenes, hoping no more
That to the highest place he might attain,
And ill content with second honors, yet
    He seemed to be a fiery thunderbolt:
Let Aeschines report, who, hearing, knew
His own voice faint beside that mighty voice.
    I cannot rightly and in order tell
Where 'twas, or when, I saw this man or that,
Or who came first and who came afterward.
    For, thinking of innumerable things,
And gazing at the great and noble throng,
My eyes and thoughts were straying constantly.

Solon I saw, who nursed the useful plant
That, if it be ill tended, bears but ill:
And the six sages of whom Greece is proud.

Leading the company of our land, I saw
Varro, the third of the great lights of Rome,
Who shines the more, the more you gaze at him;

Crispus Sallustius then; and at his side
One who held him in scorn, and envied him—
And this was Livy, the great Paduan.

While I was watching him I chanced to see
Pliny, his neighbor of Verona, who,
Wise in his writings, was unwise in death.

The Platonist Plotinus then I saw,
Who, thinking himself safe in solitude,
Was overtaken by the destiny

That had been with him ever since his birth,
So that his providence availed him nought;
Hortensius, Crassus, Galba and Antony;

Calvus and Pollio, who grew so proud
That they made wordy war on Cicero,
Seeking a fame that they did not deserve.

Thucydides I saw, who clearly tells
The times and places and the valiant deeds
Of war, and who it was that fought and bled.

I saw the father of Grecian history,
Herodotus; the great geometer,
Bedecked with circles, triangles and squares;
    Then Porphyry, a stone against our faith,
Who with the sharpness of his syllogisms
His quiver filled, and used his sophistries
    As weapons in his fight against the truth;
Hippocrates, who much advanced his art
By dicta given now but little heed;
    Before him Aesculapius and Apollo,
Shrouded so close they scarce could be discerned,
Their names hidden by time and worn away;
    Then Galen followed, who the healing art
That he found briefly stated and obscure,
Made fully clear—though it be spoiled today.
    Then Anaxarchus, manly and resolute,
Then, stronger than a rock, Xenocrates,
Who could not be compelled to a shameful act.
    Then Archimedes, with his eyes down-bent;
Democritus, absorbed in thought profound;
Who robbed himself of gold and of his sight;
    Then aged Hippias, who dared to say:
"I know all things"; and then, certain of nought,
Archesilaus, doubtful of everything;

Then Heraclitus, covert in his words;
Diogenes the cynic, covered less,
In what he did, than shame would have required;

And one who, coming home with foreign lore,
Felt himself enviable and well content
E'en though his fields were all despoiled and bare.

Here too I saw the searcher Dicaearchus,
Quintilian also, Plutarch, Seneca,
Who differed in their several masteries;

And some I saw who have disturbed the seas
With adverse winds and wanderings of mind,
Famed for contention, not for what they knew.

Like lions or like dragons did they fight
That lash with their tails: what good is there in this,
Each being well content with what he knows?

Carneades I saw, so keen of mind
And ready-tongued that when he spoke there seemed
But little difference 'twixt the true and the false.

He spent his lengthy life and his thoughtfulness
Seeking to win accord between the sects
Fiercely engaged in literary war;

But he could not prevail: as doctrines grew
So envy grew, and with the rise of learning
Diffused its poisons into swollen hearts.

'Gainst him of Syros, who raised human hopes,
Claiming the immortality of the soul,
Came Epicurus (whence his fame is less)
    Who dared to argue that it was not true—
So infamous and blinded was his light!—
And those who followed him, as Metrodorus
    And Aristippus, held to their master's thought.
Then with a marvelous spindle and weaver's beam
I saw Chrysippus weaving a subtle web.
    Antisthenes and Anaximenes
I saw, Anaximander, and then Zeno,
Now with close fist and now with open palm,
    Stating the fair opinion that he held.

THE TRIUMPH OF TIME

FORTH FROM his golden palace, after the dawn,
So swiftly rose the Sun, begirt with rays,
Thou wouldst have said: "Yet hardly had it set."

    Risen a little, he looked round about
As wise men do, and to himself he said:
"What thinkest thou? Thou shouldst take greater care.

    For if a man who had been famed in life
Continues in his fame in spite of death,
What will become of the law that heaven made?

    If mortal fame, that soon should fade away,
Increases after death, then I foresee
Our excellence at an end, wherefor I grieve.

    What more is to befall? What could be worse?
What more have I in the heavens than man on earth?
Must I then plead for equality with him?

    My four good steeds I curry faithfully,
And feed them in the seas, and spur, and lash,
And yet I yield to the fame of mortal man.

An injury for anger, not for jest,
That this should be my lot, e'en though I were
But second or third in the heavens, rather than first!
        Now must I kindle all the zeal I have
And in my wrath double my wingèd speed:
For I am envious, I confess, of men.

        For some I see who after a thousand years,
And other thousands, grow more famous still,
While I continue my perpetual task.

        I am as erst I was, ere the earth itself
Was stablished, wheeling ever, day and night,
In my round course, that never comes to an end."

        Thus did he speak; and then disdainfully
He started on again, swifter by far
Than falcon plunging downward on his prey.

        So swiftly sped he that not even thought
Could follow—and much less could tongue or pen—
So that I gazed at him in great affright.

        Watching his marvelous velocity,
This life of ours deeper in meanness seemed
Than it had once seemed high in dignity.

        An arrant vanity it now appeared
To set one's heart on things that Time may press,
For while one thinks to hold them they are gone.

Therefore let one concerned about his state
Take careful thought, while yet his will is free,
And set his hope on that which will endure.

How swiftly Time before my eyes rushed on
After the guiding Sun, that never rests,
I will not say: 'twould be beyond my power.

As in a single moment did I see
Ice and the rose, great cold and burning heat
A wondrous thing, indeed, even to hear.

But he that thoughtfully considers it
Will see it so. Why did I not, of old?
Wherefore I now am wroth against myself.

I followed then my hopes and vain desires,
But now with mine own eyes I see myself
As in a mirror, and my wanderings,

Considering now the brevity of life,
And striving to make ready for the end:
This morn I was a child, and now am old.

What more is this our life than a single day,
Cloudy and cold and short and filled with grief,
That hath no value, fair though it may seem?

Within this life men set their hope and joy
And raise their heads in miserable pride,
Yet no man knoweth when his life will end.

And now I see how fleeting is my life—
Nay more, the life of all—and in the flight
Of the Sun the manifest ruin of the world.

    Take comfort, then, in your imagined tales,
Ye that are young: give yourselves many years!
A wound that is foreseen brings lesser grief.

    It may be that I spend my words in vain,
But I declare that ye are suffering
From perilous and deadly lethargy.

    For days and hours and years and months fly on,
Nor can the time be far away when we
Must all together seek out other worlds,

    Pray harden not your hearts against the truth
As ye are wont to do; and turn your eyes
While ye may yet amend your sinful ways.

    Delay not, as most mortals do, until
Death shall transfix you with his fatal dart:
Infinite, truly, is the throng of fools.

    When I had seen, as still I clearly see,
The flying and the fleeing of the Sun,
Whence I have suffered fallacy and harm,

    I saw folk moving onward quietly,
Free from the fear of Time and of his rage,
Historians and poets guarding them.

Chiefly of these the Sun was envious:
For they, escaping from the common cage,
Had mounted upward, into soaring flight.

Against them, therefore, he who shines alone
Prepared himself his effort to increase,
Making his flight still swifter than before.

His coursers now he fed more copiously,
Striving to separate her followers
From queenly Fame, of whom I have said my say.

And then I heard a voice, and, listening, wrote:
"What dark abyss of blind oblivion
Awaits these slight and tender human flowers!

For years, for lustra, and for centuries
The Sun, victorious o'er the human mind,
Will still revolve, and Fame will fade away.

How many, famous once, are famed no more
Where rivers flow in Thrace and Thessaly,
Or by the Xanthus, or in Tiber's vale!

Your fame is nothing more than a sunlit day,
Or a doubtful winter: clouds may end it all.
Great length of time is poisonous to great names.

Your grandeur passes, and your pageantry,
Your lordships pass, your kingdoms pass; and Time
Disposes wilfully of mortal things,

And treats all men, worthy or no, alike;
And Time dissolves not only visible things,
But eloquence, and what the mind hath wrought.

And fleeing thus, it turns the world around.
Nor ever rests nor stays nor turns again
Till it has made you nought but a little dust.

Many indeed are the horns of human pride,
Nor is it strange if some of them remain,
Outlasting others, more than the common wont:

But whatsoever men may think or say,
If the span of this life of yours were not so brief,
You soon would see them fade away in smoke."

When this I heard—for to the truth we owe
No opposition, but a perfect trust—
I saw our glory melt like snow in the sun.

And I saw Time such booty bear away
That our renowns appeared as nought to me—
Although the common folk believe not so:

Blind folk, that ever dally with the wind,
Feeding on false opinions, thinking it
Better to die when old than in the cradle.

Happy are they who die in swaddling clothes,
And wretched they who die in utmost age.
"Blessed is he who is not born," 'tis said.

And even though the errant crowd may hold
That for long ages Fame may still endure,
What is it that so highly is esteemed?
    Time in his avarice steals so much away:
Men call it Fame; 'tis but a second death,
And both alike are strong beyond defense.
    Thus doth Time triumph over the world and Fame.

THE TRIUMPH OF ETERNITY

WHEN I had seen that nothing under heaven
Is firm and stable, in dismay I turned
To my heart, and asked: "Wherein hast thou thy trust?"

    "In the Lord," the answer came, "Who keepeth ever
His covenant with one who trusts in Him.
Well do I see the mockery of the world,

    And know what I have been, and what I am,
And see Time marching, nay more, flying on;
Yet there is none of whom I may complain.

    For the fault is mine: long since I should have opened
Mine eyes, instead of waiting to the end,
And true it is that I have delayed too long.

    But divine mercies never come too late:
In them I hope, that they may work in me
A transformation deep and excellent."

    'Twas thus my heart made answer. If all things
That are beneath the heavens are to fail,
How, after many circlings, will they end?

So ran my thought; and as I pondered it
More and more deeply, I at last beheld
A world made new and changeless and eternal.

 I saw the sun, the heavens, and the stars
And land and sea unmade, and made again
More beauteous and more joyous than before.

 Greatly I marveled, seeing time itself
Come to an end, that ne'er before had ceased,
But had been wont in its course to change all things.

 Past, present, future: these I saw combined
In a single term, and that unchangeable:
No swiftness now, as there had been before.

 As on an empty plain, I now could see
No "shall be" or "has been," "ne'er" or "before"
Or "after," filling life with doubtfulness.

 Thought passes as a ray of the sun through glass—
More swiftly still, for there is nought to impede.
What grace, if I am worthy, shall be mine,

 If I may there behold the Highest Good,
And none of the harm that is poured out by Time,
And comes with Time, and disappears with Time!

 The sun no more will pause in the Bull or the Fish,
Through whose diversities the work of man
Is born or dies, increases, or grows less.

Blest are the spirits who in the choir supreme
Shall be or are already honored so
That memory eternal holds their names!

Happy indeed is he who finds the ford
To cross the torrent, mountainous and swift,
That is called life, to many men so dear!

Wretched indeed the blind and common folk
Who set their hopes upon the things of earth,
That Time so suddenly doth bear away!

O truly deaf and naked and infirm,
Poor in consideration and in sense,
Ye mortals, ever miserable and ill!

Yet He who rules by motion of His brow,
Who quiets or perturbs the elements,
And to whose wisdom I may not attain—

Even the angels are content and glad
To comprehend a thousandth part of it,
And set desire and are intent thereon—

O wandering mind, ever an hunger'd still,
Wherefore so many thoughts? An hour dispels
What may be gathered in a thousand years.

All that encumbers us and weighs us down,
"Yesterday" and "tomorrow," "morn" and "eve,"
"Before" and "soon," will pass like fleeting shadows.

"Has been," "shall be," and "was" exist no more,
But "is" and "now," "the present" and "today,"
"Eternity" alone, one and complete.

Future and past, like hills that hid our view,
Are leveled now, and nothing still remains
Whereupon hope or memory may lean,

Their variation leading men astray,
Thinking "What have I been?" "What shall I be?"
As if their lives were but an empty game.

No more will time be broken into bits,
No summer now, no winter: all will be
As one, time dead, and all the world transformed.

The years no longer in their hands will hold
The governance of fame: the glorious
Will glorious be to all eternity.

Blessèd the souls that now are on the way,
Or will be soon, to reach the final goal,
Whereof I speak, whenever it may be;

And among all the rare and beauteous ones,
Most blessèd she, who long before she came
To the bound that nature sets was slain by death.

Then will be manifest the angelic modes,
The honorable words, and the chaste thoughts
That nature set within her youthful heart.

The countenances hurt by death and time
Will now appear in perfect flowering,
The bond wherewith Love bound me will be seen,
    And pointing toward me will be some who say:
"He ever wept, and yet amid his tears
Was blest above the joys of other men."
    And she of whom, still weeping, still I sing,
Will find it very wonderful that she
Should have the highest praise among them all.
    When this shall be, I know not; not to those
Who were His trusted comrades was the hour
Of death made known: who then may seek to know?
    I think the day is coming near when gains,
Both good and evil, will be judged at last,
As clearly seen as through a spider's web.
    Then 'twill appear how vain are human cares,
How uselessly we labor and we sweat,
How easily we mortals are deceived.
    No secret shall be covered or be hid,
And every conscience, be it clear or dark,
Will then be open before all the world.
    There will be One whose judgment will be sure,
And we shall see each sinner go his way
Like a driven beast seeking a forest cave.

III

Then shall we see how slight the greatness is
That we are proud of, and that gold and land
Have brought to us not benefit, but harm,
  And, at the right, those who, beneath the check
Of modest fortune, have been well content
To live without display, in homely peace.
  Five of these Triumphs on the earth below
We have beheld, and at the end, the sixth,
God willing, we shall see in heaven above.
  Time, ever ready to destroy all things,
And Death, so greedy in her evil power,
One and the other, shall together die.
  And those who merited illustrious fame
That Time had quenched, and countenances fair
Made pale and wan by Time and bitter Death,
  Becoming still more beauteous than before
Will leave to raging Death and thieving Time
Oblivion, and aspects dark and sad.
  In the full flower of youth they shall possess
Immortal beauty and eternal fame.
Before them all, who go to be made new,
  Is she for whom the world is weeping still,
Calling her with my tongue and weary pen,
But heaven too desires her, body and soul.

Beside a stream that rises in the Alps
Love gave to me for her a war so long
My heart still bears the memory thereof.
　　Happy the stone that covers her fair face!
And now that she her beauty hath resumed,
If he was blest who saw her here on earth,
　　What then will it be to see her again in heaven!